A PERSONAL JOURNAL

RUNNING PRESS
PHILADELPHIA · LONDON

9 8 7 6 4 3 2 1
Digit on the right indicates the number of this printing

ISBN 0-7624-1467-7

Illustrations © 2002 by Tinou Le Joly Senoville
Chinese character on cover by Miyako Taguchi
Cover designed by Bill Jones
Interior designed by Amanda Richmond
Edited by Deborah Grandinetti
Typography: Charme and Sabon

This book may be ordered by mail from the publisher.
Please include $2.50 for postage and handling.
But try your bookstore first!

Running Press Book Publishers
125 South Twenty-second street
Philadelphia, Pennsylvania 19103-4399

Visit us on the web!
www.runningpress.com

About The Zen Notebook

This journal introduces you to a core teaching in Buddhism—and gives you the space to contemplate its relevance in your own life. The Eightfold Path is, very simply, a systematic guide to living in a way that will bring self-understanding, peace, and ultimately, enlightenment. Think of it as the Buddha's "prescription" for eliminating the root causes of human suffering.

There are eight guiding principles, each of which flow logically out of each other. You'll find a brief explanation of each on the pages ahead, plus quotes to inspire you as you journal your way to nirvana!

Facets of The Eightfold Path:

•Right Understanding •Right Mindedness

•Right Speech •Right Action •Right Living

•Right Effort •Right Attentiveness •Right Concentration

Right Understanding

To have right understanding means to view the world exactly as it presents itself to the eye. That means seeing without imposing any preconceived notions upon what you see. There's often the temptation to categorize things too quickly, and to miss what's actually there. Buddhism challenges its students to experience everything with a clear, objective mind—so they may view people and events as they actually are.

Right Understanding

Reality as it is becomes the right view of the meditator.
Thinking of it as it is becomes the right thought.
Awareness of it as it is becomes the right awareness.
Concentration becomes the right concentration.
Actions of body and speech are then aligned to reality as it is.
In this way, the meditator develops and is fulfilled.

MAJHIMA NIKAYA

Right Understanding

*The pureness of perfectly balanced action based on seeing
the way things are—this is freedom and the ending of ignorance.*

SUTTA NIPATA

Right Understanding

Subhutu asked:
        What does buddha mean?
The Buddha answered:
        "Buddha is reality. One who thoroughly
comprehends all factors of existence is a buddha."

Right Understanding

Things are not as they seem—and nor are they otherwise.
LANKAVATARA SUTRA

Right Understanding

It is not our preferences that cause problems but our attachment to them.
BUDDHA

Right Mindedness

From *Right Understanding* flows *Right Mindedness* or *Right Thinking*—counsel meant to be applied to one's attitudes and approach toward life. Buddhism asks its students to cultivate purity of motive, and to refrain from thoughts motivated by lust, ill will, or a desire to inflict cruelty. It counsels students to realize that actions based on kindness and wisdom in the mind will bring happiness, while those based on unkindness or an unwise state of mind will bring unhappiness.

Right Mindedness

All suffering in this life and others
is created by the unsubdued mind.
THE DALAI LAMA XIV

Right Mindedness

The heart is our garden, and along with each action there is an intention that is planted like a seed. We can use a sharp knife to cut someone, and if our intention is to do harm, we will be a murderer. We can perform an almost identical action, but if we are a surgeon, the intention is to heal and save a life.

JACK KORNFIELD, *IN A PATH WITH HEART*

Right Mindedness

Like a solid rock is not shaken by the wind,
so the wise are not moved by praise or blame.
BUDDHA

Right Mindedness

Do not dwell on the past, do not dream of the future.
Concentrate the mind on the present moment.
BUDDHA

Right Mindedness

It is necessary to be noble,
*   and yet take humility as a basis.*
It is necessary to be exalted,
*   and yet take modesty as a foundation.*
LAO TZU

Right Speech

Students of Buddhism are encouraged to reflect on the power of their words and the effect they have upon others. Speech, when used carelessly, tends to promulgate suffering. Students work to eradicate exaggerations, lies, detrimental comments, and frivolity in speech. They are taught to listen with awareness as they speak, mindful of the weight their words carry.

Right Speech

It is good to control your words and thoughts.

The seeker who is in control feels free and joyful.

Right Speech

The holy spend not idle words on things of desire.

FROM THE BUDDHIST TEXT, THE DHAMMAPADA

Right Speech

Displaying self-righteousness, one reveals vanity.
Praising the self, one earns no respect.
Exaggerating achievements, one cannot long endure.

LAO TZU

Right Speech

The more you talk and think about it,
the further astray you wander from the truth.
THE 3RD ZEN PATRIARCH, SENGSTAU,
AS QUOTED IN *VERSES ON THE FAITH MIND*

Right Speech

We think that words are not deeds, that they have little power and a short life, that somehow words evaporate with the breath that speaks them. But words do have power and they can live forever; and furthermore, they can heal as well as harm.

MASTER HSU YUN, IN *EMPTY CLOUD*

Right Action

Just as words have power, so do actions. Students of Buddhism learn to reflect before they act, and to refrain from any destructive or harmful actions so they do not cause harm to others, or ultimately, to themselves. Buddhism teaches that constructive actions have constructive effects, which return positively to the individual who initiated them. Destructive or hostile actions, similarly, initiate a chain of events that can cause hostility or destructive forces to be unleashed against the individual who initiated the chain of events.

Right Action

Whoever would live well,
Long lasting, bringing bliss—
Let him be generous, be calm
And cultivate the doing of good.
FROM THE *ITIVUTTAKA SUTTA*

Right Action

My daily activities are not unusual,
   I'm just naturally in harmony with them.
Grasping nothing, discarding nothing.
   Supernatural power and marvelous activity
Drawing water and carrying firewood.

LAYMAN PANG-YUN (740—808)

Right Action

For a deed to be totally pure, it must be done without any thought of reward, whether worldly or divine. It is this kind of deed which is called a "deed of no merit." And because no merit is sought, it is a deed of immeasurable merit, of infinite merit.

THICH THIEN-AN

Right Action

To squander is to destroy. To treat things with reverence and gratitude, according to their nature and purpose, is to affirm their value and life, a life in which we are all equally rooted. Wastefulness is a measure of...our alienation from all things, from their Buddha-nature, from their essential unity with us.

ROSHI PHILIP KAPLEAU, IN *THE THREE PILLARS OF ZEN*

Right Livelihood

Buddhism teaches its students to acquire work that is in keeping with their nature, and that allows them to follow the Eightfold Path, doing harm to no one. This requires self-awareness and an awareness of the impact of the workplace on society. The student of Buddhism is asked to reflect upon his or her work—the nature of the work, the work environment, and the impact of the work on society—and make constructive choices.

Right Livelihood

We make a living by what we get, but we make a life by what we give. Right livelihood is making a life, and finding our true vocation—not just making a living.

LAMA SURYA DAS

Right Livelihood

The Buddha, in his wisdom, made "right livelihood" one of the steps to enlightenment . . . Responsible work is an embodiment of love, and love is the only discipline that makes the mind whole and constant for a lifetime of effort.

THEODORE ROSZAK, IN *CHOP WOOD, CARRY WATER*

Right Livelihood

There is no easy formula for determining right and wrong livelihood, but it is essential to keep the question alive.

To return the sense of dignity and honor to manhood, we have to stop pretending that we can make a living at something that is trivial or destructive and still have sense of legitimate self-worth.

SAM KEEN

Right Livelihood

Use your meditative awareness or mindfulness
to start to make the work you do a meditation.
JACK KORNFIELD

Right Livelihood

Right Livelihood means to avoid any life that brings shame. It embodies the other seven steps along the Eightfold Path to enlightenment.
MARTI BEDDOE, FOUNDER OF RIGHT LIVELYHOODS

Right Effort

Buddhist teachers exhort their students to be diligent in doing the practices that will awaken them to their innate enlightenment. Students are instructed to keep moving forward in their realization of their true nature, and to persevere. They are also warned to avoid laziness and indulgence, which will slow their progress. According to the teachings, right effort must be nourished with constant efforts that propel the student ever forward on the pathless path of Buddhism.

Right Effort

So an ancient once said, "Accept the anxieties and difficulties of this life."
Don't expect your practice to be clear of obstacles.
Without hindrances the mind that seeks enlightenment may be burnt out.
So an ancient once said, "Attain deliverance in disturbances."

ZEN MASTER KYONG HO

Right Effort

But do not feel overwhelmed by the length of this journey.
All you ever need do is focus on one thing, what you are doing.
Stay on the path and put one foot in front of the other—that is all.
There is joy in the struggle.

P.T. Sudo

Right Effort

Sentient Beings Are Numberless, I Vow to Liberate Them
Desires are Inexhaustible, I Vow to Put an End to Them
The Dharmas Are Boundless, I Vow to Master Them
The Buddha's Way is Unsurpassable, I Vow to Become It
THE FOUR VOWS OF MAHAYANA BUDDHISM AND RINZAI ZEN

Buddhism does not have the answer to your question...
        You do. Only you do.
The answer and the question are one and the same thing.
        Zen is a process, not an answering machine.
                JOHN DAIDO LOORI IN *THE HEART OF BEING:*
                MORAL AND ETHICAL TEACHINGS OF ZEN BUDDHISM

Right Effort

To study the Path, first you must have a basis of enlightenment:
It's like having vied in a boat race:
Though you relax on idle ground as before,
only having won you can rest.

HEKIGAN ROKU

Right Attentiveness

Buddhist teachers consider an aptitude for critical thinking essential in the quest for freedom, because it allows students to recognize and acknowledge the confusion within. They teach students to use this capacity in the pursuit of self-awareness, a quality they consider valuable because it can be used to discern each and every influence that might pull one off the spiritual path. Once a student learns to discern negative influences, she is then instructed to distance herself from them until she is able to remove herself from their sway entirely.

*To be aware of a single shortcoming within oneself is
more useful than to be aware of a thousand in somebody else.*
HIS HOLINESS THE DALAI LAMA

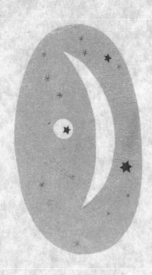

To grasp Zen, you must experience it ...
You should withdraw inwardly and search for the ground
upon which you stand; thereby you will find out what Truth is.
UMMON [YUN-MEN WEN-YEN]

Right Attentiveness

Never underestimate the potential of ego to lead one astray,
no matter how hard you train or what your point on the path.
The rush of learning a new skill, the flattery that accompanies
a touch of success—these things can overinflate any person's ego.

P.T. SUDO

Your self-partiality is at the root of all your illusions.
There aren't any illusions when you don't have this preference for yourself!
THE JAPANESE ZEN MASTER BANKEI

Right Concentration

Concentration, in this sense, is the calm but intense focus that students of Buddhism apply in spiritual practice so they may penetrate through illusion to pure awareness. When right concentration is fully applied, it allows practitioners to enter into a state of being where there is no separation between the Buddhist meditator, the act of meditation, and object of meditation. The practice of right concentration gradually allows the Buddhist practitioner to achieve deeper and deeper focus, which is necessary to penetrate through illusions to the Ultimate Reality.

Right Concentration

Zazen means to be intimate with the self.
To be intimate with the self is to realize the whole phenomenal universe at the self.
JOHN DAIDO LOORI, ABBOT, ZEN MOUNTAIN MONASTERY, MOUNT TREMPER, NEW YORK

Right Concentration

An explosive shout cracks the great empty sky.
Immediately clear self-understanding.
Swallow up buddhas and ancestors of the past.
Without following others, realize complete penetration.

DOGEN, 1200—1253

Right Concentration

So long as the winds of thought continue to disturb the
water of our Self-nature, we cannot distinguish truth from
untruth. It is imperative, therefore, that these winds be stilled.
ROSHI PHILIP KAPLEAU, IN *THE THREE PILLARS OF ZEN*

Right Concentration

In Zen, there is nothing to explain,
nothing to teach, that will add to your knowledge.
Unless it grows out of yourself, no knowledge is really
of value to you, a borrowed plumage never grows.
D.T. SUZUKI, IN ESSAYS IN ZEN BUDDHISM

Right Concentration

The Buddha Way is not about belief systems. It is about
empowering yourself, realizing yourself, finding the answer in yourself.
Your own direct experience of realization, and then actualization of
that realization in the world ... It has to flow out of your heart.
ZEN ABBOT JOHN DAIDO LOORI, IN *THE HEART OF BEING:*
MORAL AND ETHICAL TEACHINGS OF ZEN BUDDHISM